GW01111770

My Hamster

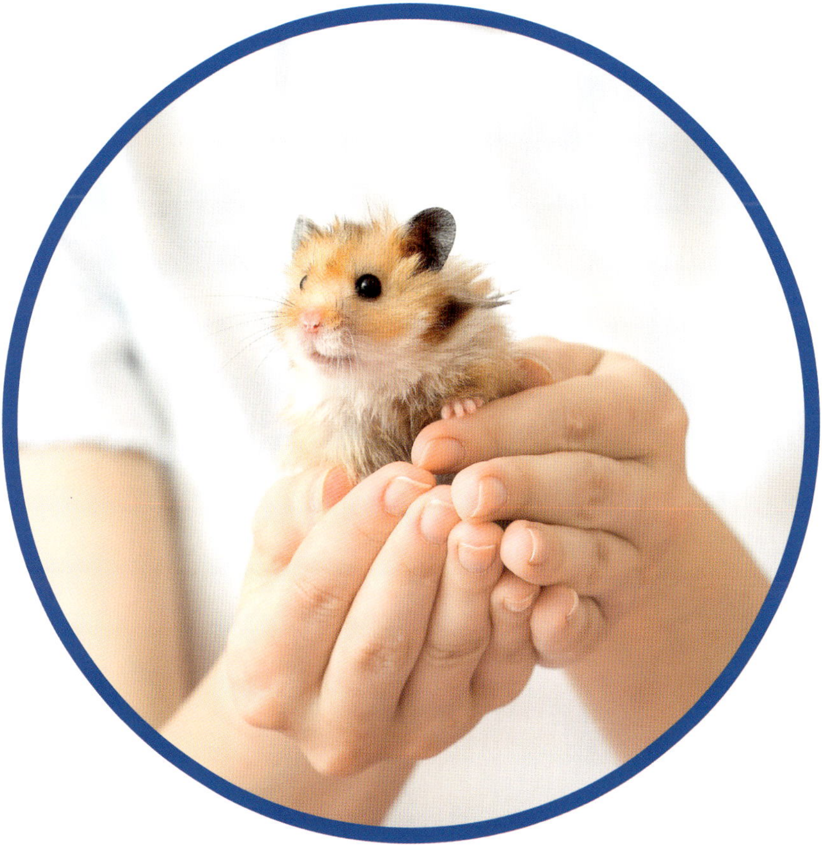

Written by
Gabriel Beveridge

This is Patty, my pet hamster.
It is my job to take care of her.

Hamsters need a safe and homely habitat to live in. Patty likes to burrow in wood shavings, so I spread them around her home.

Patty needs a fresh drink and fresh food each day. Hamsters mostly eat seeds and grains.

Hamsters are active animals and like to run around. They will be sad if they do not have much to do.

Patty has a hamster wheel to run on. She likes to run in the wheel and make it spin as quickly as she can.

She likes to eat lots of things. I gave her a pinecone today and she really liked it.
We only give her new foods if the vet tells us they are safe for her to eat.

My sister keeps feeding her bread, but it is not good for her health! Hamsters are not meant to eat food made for humans.

As a treat, Patty gets one carrot stick each week. She thinks that carrot sticks are the best thing ever.

She likes to stash it away so she can have some later.

Sometimes she forgets to eat it and I have to clean it up. If I don't, it will start to rot.

Patty likes being petted. However, my friends don't understand that Patty has to be petted very lightly. If you are cuddling her too tightly, you might crush her.

She needs to be held with both hands. She enjoys a soft pat on the top of her head.

Patty is very cute, but she needs a lot of care.

 Can you spot these details in the book?

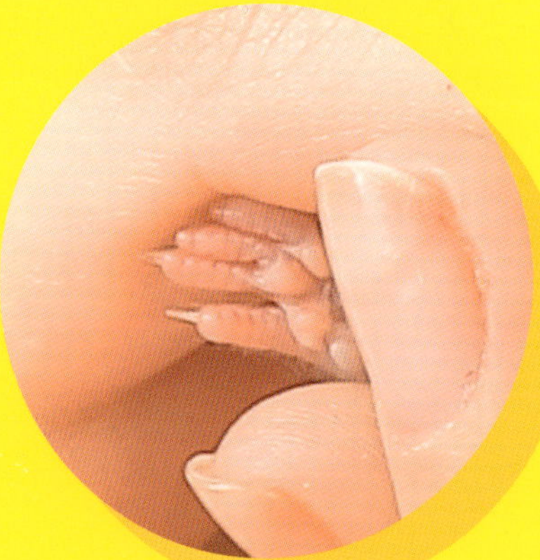